Finding W
Harmony and Rest

Exposing the Conflict in All Thinking

Darryl Bailey

New Sarum Press
United Kingdom

FINDING WHOLENESS, HARMONY AND REST
Copyright ©Darryl Bailey 2021
Copyright ©New Sarum Press 2021

All rights reserved. No part of this book may be reproduced or transmitted in any form or by any means, electronic or mechanical, including photocopying, recording, or any information storage and retrieval system, without permission in writing from the author.

Front cover image adapted from a painting by Darryl Bailey
Layout and cover design: Julian Noyce

ISBN: 978-1-8383836-3-3

Contents

Preface v

1. Life's Greatest Difficulty 1
2. The Major Conflict in Human Existence 19
3. The Delusion in Detail 25
4. The Way Out of Delusion 36
5. How Can We Live Without Thinking? 46

Endnote 57
Acknowledgments 59

Preface

What I'm offering in this work is a radically different view of our life, and a radically different view of our thinking process, radically different to the views that most people have.

This presentation is meant to be considered in relation to your experience of life. It's not a theory to be debated intellectually. It's a consideration of your actual experience and what that experience indicates.

Many of you will feel that this work is a very clear pointing to life as you experience it. Many of you won't. I'm simply offering it for your consideration.

Whatever your response is to this presentation, I respect that you are your own unique being, and I wish you well in your particular life journey.

Life's Greatest Difficulty

I want to consider a major difficulty that arises in the life of every person, and within society in general. It is perhaps the single largest barrier to the happiness and health of every human being and the largest barrier to the happiness and health of society as a whole.

This difficulty has to do with the relationship of thinking to our actual experience of existence, and the fact that every thought that we have is in conflict with our experience of life.

Let me repeat that statement: every thought that we have is in conflict with the life that we experience.

Every thought is a confused assessment of life, an assessment inherently filled with delusion, fragmentation, conflict, and struggle.

But before we discuss the delusion and conflict that is inherent in all thinking, I want to consider three simple facts about our life.

1. Existence is the happening of this moment

If I ask you why you feel that you are existing, you would say it's because it feels like something is happening right now.

That's our only feeling of existing, the feeling that something is happening right now.

You don't have to create the feeling that something is happening. In fact, you can't get away from it. Right now, it feels like something is happening.

Try shutting your eyes for a few minutes, and simply feel the happening that you are. Feel the warm, vibrant happening that you are.

You don't have to think about it, just feel it.

You don't have to make any effort in this. It feels like something is happening, so simply close your eyes and feel it.

When your eyes are open again, it feels like the bigger happening of the moment. So now, with your eyes open, feel the full happening of this moment, for a few minutes.

After that, again close your eyes and feel the warm happening that you are.

When your eyes are open again, if you can, try feeling the happening of seeing.

Don't focus on one small part of the field of seeing—instead, feel the complete happening that we call seeing.

Don't call it anything, just feel it.

This may seem a bit odd, to feel the happening that we call seeing, but you'll find that you can feel it.

And now, once again, feel the complete happening of this moment. What you call the inside of you and the outside of you, combined, simply feel the entire happening of this moment.

Now that we have a clearer sense of this immediate happening of life, I want to consider a few other things.

2. There is no way of saying what this happening is

If I ask you what this happening of the moment is, you really have no way of saying what it is.

The feeling that something is happening is what starts at birth. Babies have the same basic feeling that you do, the feeling that something is happening, right now, but babies don't know what this happening is. Babies aren't born with words, or labels, for anything.

If you ask a newborn baby, "What's happening right now?", the baby isn't going to say anything. The baby can't even understand a question.

But it's obvious that the baby has the feeling that something is happening. Any baby has the same basic feeling that you have, the feeling that something is happening right now. But a baby has no words for it, no names.

For the baby, it's a totally unexplainable happening. There is the feeling that something is happening, but there are no words for it, no thoughts about it.

As adults, we have endless names for the happening of this moment. We call it awareness, a self, a world, existence, the universe, and we name a million other things: thoughts, moods, bodies, trees, houses, people, planets, stars, and so on.

If we consider this carefully, we can realise that we've been taught to point to different portions of the happening of this moment, by using different words.

If we lived in another country, where a different language is spoken, we would be taught different labels.

The important thing to realise is that the words aren't telling us what this happening is. The words just point to different portions of the happening.

If we wanted to, we could use words like "buzzleboot" and "windyshout", instead of words like "awareness" and "body", to point to different bits of this happening.

It's important to see that words like awareness and body don't tell us what anything actually is, they are simply pointers.

When the words point to a certain portion of this happening, we call that portion a "thing".

We point to one shape and call it a wall, another shape, a floor, and another shape we call a body. Sometimes the shapes are very vague, like the shape we call a thought, or a mood, but we feel there is a shape, or pattern, of some kind, and we give it a name.

We point to every shape, form, and pattern that we can possibly find, giving them names, and calling them "things".

It's important to realise that, in our experience of life, every "thing" is changing.

Everyone eventually says that, in their experience, everything is changing.

It's obvious that things like thoughts and moods change quickly; bodies and relationships change slowly; mountains, galaxies, and the universe, change even more slowly; but everyone agrees that they are all changing. Every so-called "thing" is changing.

For people who study it very closely, like the physicists, they say that everything is changing all the time, in gross and subtle ways, so everything is really a process of movement.

Quantum physicists generally say there are no actual things, there is only process, movement, action, or flow.

They experience existence as the flow of something they call energy.

This is the same basic fact that a fellow named Ashtavakra declared, twenty-eight hundred years ago, when, in the *Ashtavakra Gita*, he stated that all things are like waves moving in an ocean, that all things are really like the unformed, flowing movement of water.

This is also what the Greek philosopher, Heraclitus, was pointing to, twenty-five hundred years ago, when he stated that life is simply flowing like a river, always changing, never the same from moment to moment.

This is what Jesus was saying, two thousand years ago, when he said there is only spirit, something that has no form. He said it's like the blowing of the wind, or the flowing of waters. He equated spirit with what he called the waters of life.

The early Chinese Taoists also stated that everything in life is flowing like a stream of water, and there is only the way that it flows. The word Tao means the Way, the way that everything flows.

The Buddha, too, stated that life is an unformed happening, that it is like the flowing of a river, never pausing for a moment, or an instant, or a second.

James Joyce, the true master of words, said it most succinctly, when he stated that "Finnegans Wake". He was simply pointing out that what seems to be the arising and passing of finite forms, again and again, "fin agains", are actually an unformed flowing, like a wave in water, a "wake" behind a boat. "Fin Agains Wake" is simply saying that all apparent things are actually flowing like water.

Philosophers, from times earlier than Ashtavakra, up through to Buddha and Jesus, then on to more recent times, with Nietzsche, Whitehead, Heidegger, and a myriad of others, including physicists, like the impeccable David Bohm, have been pointing to this same simple fact of change and flow, throughout all of history.

And so has everyone else.

Every adult person that you know of will probably agree that everything is changing. That's our most commonly shared experience of life.

You don't have to focus on a lifetime of experience, or teachings from history, in order to experience this. You can simply feel it in the happening of this moment.

If we sit down and do nothing, if we simply feel the happening of this moment, we find a warm, vibrant, shifting occurrence, making itself obvious.

If you sit quietly, doing nothing, you'll discover that the happening of this moment, the happening that you are, is a moving, shifting, vibrant, event.

There is the feeling of the breath coming and going, the heart beating, the tingling of the body, vibrations, pulsations, waves of energy, heat and coolness, tightness, looseness, heaviness, lightness, a little twinge here, a little shift there, sounds coming and going, thoughts coming and going, moods coming and going, and so on. If the eyes are closed, there is the dance of light and dark, in what we call seeing. If the eyes are open, there is the movement of the eyes and the shifting of the entire field of seeing. If the sitting feels pleasant, there is an urge to remain sitting. If it is unpleasant, there is an urge to move and shift and maybe stand up. Eventually we will be compelled to stand up and go on to other activities.

All of this reveals itself clearly, when we simply sit quietly, doing nothing.

The Buddha asked us to sit quietly, to meditate, to feel the warm, vibrant, moving, shifting occurrence of the moment. To experience the simple, vibrant, unformed happening that we are, that life is.

Jesus pointed out that we are spirit, like the flowing of water, and that, if you go some place private, and sit quietly, you will find the waters of life flowing inside you.

Whether it was Buddha, Jesus, the Taoists, or anyone else considering the actual fact of our experience, they were always pointing to this fact of change, movement, and action … the warm flow of this moment.

If we consider this thoroughly, what we actually experience, we can realise that everything is changing. Every thing has a beginning, a changing, and a fading away. Thoughts, moods, bodies, people, houses, plants, animals, weather, cities, planets, galaxies, and so on, all things come and go, moving, shifting and changing. Some of it changes quickly and some of it changes slowly, but all of it is simply a changing, flowing event. As the Buddha once said, even the earth itself will someday be gone.

So, in our actual experience, life is the immediate, vibrant happening of this moment, and this happening has no particular form or shape.

There is no way to say what anything really is, because it has no real name and it has no real shape, or form, that we can possibly describe. It's a movement of some kind.

It's the constant absence of form, which we sometimes call flowing.

But a word is never the happening that it points to.

The word chair is not what it points to. Write the word chair on a piece of paper and put it on the happening that we call a chair. Then take that paper and place it next to the happening that we call a chair. You can easily see that the word is not the thing that it is pointing to.

When we see that the happening of this moment has no real name and it has no real form to be described, we can say that it is without form. It is a dynamic action, which we sometimes call flow. But the word flow is not the happening itself.

It's important to note that this is not saying that life is formless. Ideas of form and formlessness don't really apply to what's happening.

We can move beyond the ideas of form and formlessness, to words like movement, action, or flow, but even those labels are still not the actual happening.

Ultimately, there is only what feels like the happening of this moment, with no possible way of saying what it really is.

The strangest aspect, of all of this, is that every one of us has the same basic experience of life that Buddha, Jesus, the Taoists, and the physicists have had, but we don't make the very simple, and obvious, comments about it that they do.

They say that, in their experience of life, everything is changing, so there really are no things, there is only change, movement, or action, that has the appearance of form, but is really more like the movement of water, the wind, the clouds, and so on.

We have that same basic experience, that everything is changing. Yet, when someone asks us what life is all about, we give endless descriptions of people and things, endless stories about static, unchanging shapes.

Don't you think that's strange?

Because, if we say that everything is changing, that must mean that life, as we experience it, is a movement, a flowing, shifting dynamic, that can't really be described, because it has no real shape that can ever be described.

But we don't say that. We say it's a bunch of static things that can be described in infinite detail.

That's like taking a still photograph of moving smoke and then telling everyone that the still photograph really shows the movement of smoke, as it actually is. That makes no sense.

If we are to really point to the happening of this moment, it makes more sense to say that it is a changing dynamic, a movement, an action, a flow that has no actual form, or shape.

Every apparent form, or thing, is changing. So, life, the immediate happening of this moment, is more accurately pointed to as movement or action, the action of creation, endlessly forming itself into something new. Endlessly becoming, and so never really becoming anything in particular. This moment is an endless becoming that is beyond words and language.

That's how Nietzsche described it and I would agree.

We could call it the great spirit, or the river of life, or the unformed ocean of existence.

So, life, the happening of this moment, appears to have form, but if we consider it closely, it actually has no form. And it has no actual name.

If we want to discover what life really is, there is just the feeling of the warm, vibrant happening of this moment, and no possible way of saying what it is.

3. There is no one making anything happen

Another important aspect of the happening of this moment is the fact that no one is making anything happen.

Right now, it feels like you are happening. The entire process that you are is happening. It feels like you are happening right now.

What are you doing to make yourself happen?

Sit down, or lie down, and make no effort to do anything at all. Just rest. What you will discover is that you still go on happening. Everything that you are happens, without you making any effort at all.

As you are resting, ask yourself, "What am I doing to make myself happen?" Ask the question and then simply feel the happening that you are.

Does it feel like you are making yourself happen? Or are you simply happening?

Sitting quietly, doing nothing, everything continues to happen. The process that you are continues to happen, and the process of the world around you continues to happen.

As the old Zen poem states, "Sitting quietly, doing nothing, spring comes, grass grows by itself."

We can see that everything simply happens by itself. The seasons change, the weather shifts, plants grow, animals evolve, the sun moves through the sky, the moon rises at night, and so on. We call this the movement of nature, or the movement of the universe, and we all have the experience that it happens automatically.

We don't have the impression that a planet is deciding to be the planet that it is or that it's deciding how it's going to move. We don't have the feeling that the weather is deciding what it's going to be or what it's going to do. We don't have the feeling that a squirrel is deciding what it's going to be or what it's going to do. We have the feeling that everything is a movement of nature and everything occurs according to the forces of nature that give rise to the natural world.

And nature is an expression of the larger movement of the universe. The word universe, in its most ancient meaning, means "one turning". One big movement.

We believe that everything in existence is an expression of the universe, an expression of nature. Birds and flowers don't make themselves happen. They are expressions of nature and they are always the only thing that they can be in any moment.

We don't have the impression that they are making themselves happen or that they are deciding to be what they are. They simply happen as expressions of nature. This is obvious to all of us.

It's also obvious that this movement of nature has its own natural order.

We don't criticize the way the stars are arranged in the night sky and we don't tell a daisy that it should be something else. We have the feeling that everything is the natural expression of the universe, and it is always the only thing that it can be in any moment. It is always the correct expression of nature, the universe.

The early Taoists pointed very strongly to this natural flow of nature. Science also generally points to the natural laws, or movement, of the universe.

In more recent times, the pioneering therapist Carl Rogers pointed to what he called the actualising tendency. This tendency is the urge in the universe to move in a certain way. In each moment, everything is simply becoming what it has to be, because the universe has a natural urge to express itself in a certain way, to actualise, or manifest, in a certain way, in each moment.

We could call this a formative urge, because, even though existence doesn't have any real form, it has the appearance of passing forms, and they arise and pass in a certain way. Existence always has an urge to form itself in a certain way.

The movement of nature automatically expresses itself as plants, animals, weather conditions, stars, and everything else that we can identify.

The plants, animals, weather conditions, and stars aren't making themselves happen. They simply happen the way they happen, because the movement of life has a built-in urge to happen that way.

We don't tell a small tree that, if it had tried harder, it could have been a big tree, and we wouldn't tell a beetle that it has failed, because, if it had tried harder, it could have been a butterfly.

That would make no sense.

Instead, we honour all of the expressions of nature as being true and natural expressions of existence and for being the amazingly exotic and unique expressions that they are.

Each expression of nature is unique, each apparent form is different from every other apparent form.

No two trees, no two leaves, no two snowflakes, no two people, are identical. No two anything are identical. They can sometimes be very similar, but they can never be identical. We marvel at all of the expressions of nature. We marvel at the big, mysterious event that it is, appreciating the wonder of it, the mystery of it, and the beauty of it. We see everything in this way.

Everything.

Except for one thing ... us ... human beings. For some reason, we don't see ourselves as expressions of nature.

We believe that we create ourselves. We believe that we decide what we will be, and what we will do, in life.

In other words, we believe that we operate separately from the forces of nature and that we influence the movement of the universe. We believe that we move the universe.

Let's be clear about this point. We generally believe that we direct the world around us, that we control ourselves and the world.

This belief has puzzled many people throughout the ages, because it makes no sense. The philosopher Schopenhauer pointed to the simple fact that we can do what we want to do, but we don't create our wants.

No one ever creates their wants, in any moment. Our wants are given by nature.

Einstein read Schopenhauer's statement, at the age of seventeen, and realised that we are simply an expression of the universe, like rocks, trees and stars, and that we do not direct the course of our life any more than a stone, or a tomato plant, directs its existence.

The Buddha pointed out that there is no experience of a "self" that is separate from the movement of life. In everything that we experience, there is no experience of a self that is making anything happen.

Jesus would ask people, "What do the birds and flowers do, to be what they are or to get what they get in life?" I've paraphrased his question, but that was the question.

And the answer is simple. Nothing.

Birds and flowers don't do anything, to be what they are, or to get what they get in life; they are simply expressions of nature. They don't create themselves, or their behaviour.

Jesus would then ask, "Why do you think it's different for human beings?"

So again, sit down and rest for a moment. Make no effort to do anything and see what happens. Do you stop happening? Or do you continue to happen, automatically?

Again, if you simply sit, or lie down, and rest, the warm, vibrant occurrence that you are makes itself obvious. Breath comes and goes, thoughts come and go, moods, sounds, pulsations, vibrations, and so on move and shift on their own and, at some point, you will be compelled to stand up and participate in other activities, none of which you make happen.

There is no experience, anywhere, of us making anything happen.

Life, as we actually experience it, is simply the warm,

vibrant happening of this moment and we are not making it happen.

This moment is a creative movement, an endless becoming that never becomes anything in particular.

To know ourselves, and existence, in the fullest, truest way is to simply feel this happening, happening on its own. We are this immediate happening. That's all that ever exists. It is not something that can be understood and it is not something that is being "done". Nothing in this moment is being understood, and nothing in this moment is being done by a "self".

The Major Conflict in Human Existence

So now we come to the major difficulty in our life.

The difficulty is the strange belief that we are something called a "self" that is understanding and directing existence.

We generally believe that our descriptions of life are true and, from that true understanding, we believe that we are directing our own existence and the existence of the world around us. Instead of examining our experience of life in a clear way, and realising that the descriptions of a "self", a "world", and "personal doing", can't possibly be true, we generally assume that they are true.

Because we ignore our actual experience of life, ignoring the warm, vibrant, unexplainable happening of this moment, we focus, instead, on deluded thinking, the fantasies of a self, a world, and personal doing.

Because we falsely believe that we are understanding and directing life, we always want life to be something other than what it is, believing that we can make it better.

So, we attempt to change our existence, attempting to create a better world, a better universe.

The difficulty with this is that there is no self that is understanding or directing existence.

All of that is a fantasy. It doesn't exist.

And the result of this deluded fantasy is endless conflict, conflict with life as it actually is, and how it naturally expresses itself. We are constantly attempting to stop the natural order, the natural flow of life.

This is a constant mental argument with the natural expressions of life, the natural, and true, expressions of existence.

It is the constantly frustrating attempt to change life into something other than what it is, in every moment.

Because we don't really exist as anything that is influencing the movement of life, the constant attempt to change life into something other than what it is, only results in extreme frustration and despair.

Because we believe that we can change ourselves into something better, and that everyone else can do the same, we always condemn ourselves, and others, for not being better than what we are.

Because we don't exist as something that can direct its own existence, we always fail to change life into what we want it to be, and, in the frustration of that failure, we attempt to increase our ability to control everything, in more violent ways.

As the frustration of failure increases, and the attempt to gain control increases, there is a growing attitude of violence towards oneself and towards others in society. Individuals, and society, then lose their ability to live in any harmonious way.

All of this conflict, and violence, stems from one simple fact: we believe that we are something separate from life, something that is understanding and directing life. We believe that we control life, that we influence life. This is a massive delusion. It's not true.

The delusion, the mistaken belief that we are understanding and directing existence, and the refusal to explore that delusion, is a situation of ever-growing confusion, conflict, and emotional despair.

When we feel the painful frustration that comes from trying to control everything in life and not being able to control it, and feel the despair of wanting everything to be different, but not getting it to be different, we want that pain and despair to stop.

So, we try to understand life better, with more thinking, and make stronger efforts to control everything.

But it's the deluded fantasy that we are understanding life, through thinking, and the fantasy that we are controlling existence, that is causing the frustration, pain and conflict, in the first place. So, increasing the focus on thinking, and the idea of control, just makes everything worse.

The actual way out of the conflict is to explore our life, to see that thinking is creating a fantasy that is always in conflict with our life as it actually is.

If we consider life clearly, and realise the conflicted delusions in the thinking process, the focus may come off those delusions and come back to what we really are, the simple, warm, vibrant occurrence of this moment, always happening in its full and natural way.

We may stop focusing on thought, if we see, very clearly, that all thinking is a conflicted, painful fantasy. It is never telling us what life really is. The obsessive focus on thinking may end, when it is realised that all thinking is deluded, conflicted, and false; all thinking creates confusion and pain.

The highest harmony, and order, of existence is not found in thinking. It's not found in the deluded notions of understanding and directing life.

The deluded belief that we are understanding, and directing, life is an extreme contradiction to the fact that we have no possible way of understanding life and we are not making any of it happen.

Every thought is in conflict with our actual experience of life.

The descriptions created with thought, the descriptions of form and the stories of a self that is separate from life, a self that is directing life, are absolute fantasies that bring only frustration and emotional pain.

In realising this clearly, we may come to realise that life is only the simple, warm, vibrant happening of this moment, realising that there is no way to say what it is and no one is making anything happen.

Everything in life is simply given. It simply happens.

As it says in the Bible, we are living in a garden where everything is given, and we are driven out of that garden when we eat of the tree of knowledge, the process of thinking.

In focusing on thinking, we lose sight of the simple happening of our experience, the fact that everything is simply the warm, vibrant, unexplainable, unforming occurrence of this moment.

When we focus on thinking, we lose reality, because all thinking is a deluded assessment of our experience.

If we examine the distorted views that all thinking contains, and see the delusions that it contains, we can let go of the focus on those delusions and simply feel what we really are, the warm, vibrant happening of this moment, without knowing what it is, without making it happen.

We can then remain clear about the simple happening that life is, the feeling of this happening, without falling prey to illusions of thought, the delusions of understanding and control, and the painful frustration and emotional despair that comes with those delusions.

The Delusion in Detail

I want to now consider the delusion of thinking in a more detailed way.

It is a complex delusion, with some very subtle aspects, but I will do my best to focus on the essentials of it.

Both the Buddha and modern researchers into child development have described the unfolding of conceptual viewpoints in a very similar way, a general way, but I want to explore certain points in greater detail.

So, let's begin.

We've already established that anyone who investigates life carefully comes to realise that, in their actual experience, life has no form. Everything is changing. But most people believe that life is made up of various forms, or things, so how does that occur?

As newborns, we have no ideas about life. There is the feeling that something is happening, but there is no story for any of it, no understanding of what it is.

The fact that everything is changing will become more obvious, as we grow older, but life appears to have various shapes and forms, and many of those shapes and forms change very slowly; they appear to be unchanging.

When we are infants, those forms appear to be static and unchanging, so we begin to interpret life in terms of form.

There is a natural urge in the happening that we are to search for every shape, form, and pattern that we can possibly find.

Let's be clear about this process, because this is the most basic delusion that makes all other thinking deluded.

Ignorance of the fact that life is always changing, moving, shifting, and flowing gives rise to the deluded belief that life has form, and the belief that the process of identifying and naming form is a true understanding of existence.

With that essential delusion, we begin to identify every shape, form, and pattern that we possibly can.

We don't simply feel the warm, vibrant, flowing that we are, that existence actually is. Instead, we begin to mentally divide this flowing into all of its appearances of shape, form, and pattern.

This identification of shapes, forms, and patterns doesn't happen in any particular order; it arises as one big event, and we begin identifying shapes, forms, and patterns anywhere we can.

This doesn't happen in any particular order, but it does have certain stages.

Initially, we can't identify form. The eyes need to develop the ability to trace the full outline of a shape, in order to identify that form, and that development takes, on average, about two months to develop.

Even when we are able to see the basic shapes and forms that life appears to have, we still aren't able see those shapes and forms as permanent things.

The actual experience of the moment is always changing in some way, and, as infants, we don't have the ability to remember the similarities of one moment to the next. We need memory to develop, in order to remember the similarities of one moment to the next.

For example, if a child looks at a moving hand and doesn't have the ability to remember anything, the moving hand looks different in each moment; it's not the same thing from moment to moment.

However, once memory develops, the child remembers certain aspects of this movement that look similar in each moment. We begin to focus on the similarities and ignore the differences.

In the case of a moving hand, we begin to focus on the fact that the movement always seems to have a general pattern of one oval shape with five other shapes sticking out of it. Even though it is really always moving, shifting and changing, there is a similar, general pattern in the movement, the general appearance of a large shape, with five smaller shapes sticking out of it.

We become fascinated with that similarity and start to see the moving, shifting flow as one constant "thing" that is always there. And we call that thing a hand.

This is a gradual development and it takes somewhere between eight to twelve months for the notion of a permanent "thing" to develop.

This inclination to ignore the fact that everything is changing, from moment to moment, and to focus only on general similarities, from one moment to the next, begins to function in all areas of our experience.

Again, this identifying process has no specific order to it, we simply identify any general shape and pattern that we can, and begin thinking of them as constant, unchanging "things". So, let's consider some of the things that we create in this false idea of permanence.

The feeling that something is happening in this moment can be divided into six basic patterns that we call seeing, hearing, touching, tasting, smelling, and, eventually, thinking.

We can also identify smaller shapes, forms, and patterns, within each of those larger sections. For example, what we call "seeing" is a big happening that can be divided into smaller portions that we call "objects" of seeing.

It's important to note an amazing illusion that occurs in this identifying process.

We can focus on the big happening that we call "seeing". Then the focus can come off that big happening and focus on one small part of the happening, like a shape we call a chair, and we can call that an "object of seeing".

Then we say that they are two separate things.

But that's like looking at a cloud and then looking at one small part of the same cloud, and saying that they are two separate things.

People seldom realise that when they are seeing a chair, it is not a situation of two things; it's not "seeing" and an "object of seeing".

It's one happening, being focused on in two different ways, being given two different names, and then being interpreted as two totally separate things.

This same illusion occurs in the other patterns we call hearing, touching, tasting, smelling and, eventually, thinking.

There is the basic feeling that something is happening, right now, and we mentally divide that happening into six portions that we call seeing, hearing, touching, tasting, smelling, and thinking. Then each of those happenings has the illusion of being two separate things.

In this delusion of separation, we get the impression that there is an awareness being aware of a world that is separate from it.

We get the impression that this awareness, this consciousness, is perceiving the shapes and forms of a world in an accurate way.

This is an absolute fantasy, an illusion, but, for all of us, in the first portion of our lives, it seems to be the truth.

In actuality, there is only one, undivided happening, but it seems to be a bunch of separate things.

One of the shapes, forms, and patterns that we can identify will eventually be called "my body", because the shape of that body seems to be closer than all the other shapes and forms.

The idea of that body becomes associated with the idea of awareness, and there is the belief that the body has awareness.

These false interpretations of form are combined, to become the story of an awareness, in a body, that is separate from all other things in the world.

As this false interpretation of a body, and other forms, is developing, there are also patterns of that body connecting with other shapes and forms, so this eventually becomes the story of our body "contacting" other things in the world.

In identifying contact with other objects, there are more subtle patterns that we will call the feelings of pleasure, displeasure, and neutral feelings.

There is a natural urge, within the process that we are, to enjoy pleasant feelings and to dislike unpleasant, or neutral, boring feelings. So the moment the focus goes on patterns that we call feelings, there is an incredible urge to cling to pleasant feelings and that urge triggers actions to maintain the pleasure. Researchers into child development call these repeated actions, or behaviours, "circular reactions".

Let's consider what has happened thus far.

The warm, vibrant happening of this moment, that has no actual form, is being looked upon as having stable forms that can be identified.

In that mental viewpoint, the unformed happening of this moment is being interpreted as an awareness, inside a body, that is coming into contact with other things, and experiencing pleasant feelings.

There is a natural compulsion to cling to pleasant feelings, so this stimulates an automatic, physical response, to cling to any pleasant activity.

Now we come to a big problem.

Everything is actually changing, so the situations that produce the pleasure will change, and we lose the pleasure. If we're trying to cling to that pleasure, there will be a problem.

In the development of every child, this is a psychological catastrophe, a disaster of immense proportions.

Prior to this point, a baby's activities are random, wandering from one activity to another, with no difficulty.

Once the focus goes on pleasure, and there is enough memory to remember pleasure, we cling to that pleasure, so now there is a huge explosion, if that pleasure is taken away.

If the object of pleasure is taken away, the excited energy that is built up in feeling the pleasure, gets frustrated, and that energy spills into neurological pathways that cause a physical disruption in the body. The baby then kicks, flails its arms, and cries.

So now, the process that we are is resisting the movement of life. And this resistance surfaces in every aspect of our lives.

By the age of eight, we will have the solid belief that we are an awareness, in a body, that is controlling and directing the world around it. When this first develops, it is simply a baby wanting something pleasant. As this delusion continues to maintain itself, and develops further, it becomes adult behaviour wanting to control every aspect of life, both in one's own being, and in the world around us.

No matter how much existence reveals that we do not have control over life, we want control, and in the frustration of losing the things we want, or not getting the things we want, we become even more determined to get control, often in violent ways.

Initially, we do this with a strong controlling attitude, towards our own life and the lives of others, but that often escalates to violent attempts to control life.

The range of attempted control is large. It can be any number of behaviours. It can be something as simple as an individual always wishing that they were someone different, or it can be something more extreme, such as someone becoming so frustrated with who they are that they commit suicide.

It could be a husband, or wife, trying to control their partner. Or it can be special interest groups fighting in the streets, or a fascist dictatorship attempting to control the lives of millions of people.

All of that mental, and physical, behaviour is coming from this deluded fantasy that we are controlling existence.

We want to make life better in whatever way we think better is. It's always the notion that life would be better if it was exactly the way that we want it to be.

So, we always want life to be something other than what it is, deludedly thinking that we are directing existence, deludedly thinking that we control life.

But all of this is a fantasy.

There is no self that is separate from the movement of life. There is no self making anything happen.

There is simply the fantasy of a self that is in control, and that fantasy is constantly being frustrated, when it can't get life to be what it wants it to be.

In general, we don't seem to have the ability to move beyond that fantasy. Instead, we maintain the fantasy, and the frustrating struggle that it contains. For most people, this deluded struggle simply increases, and often intensifies, to a level of despair.

This is a struggle with the natural flow of life. We are constantly attempting to impose the wants of an imaginary self on the flow of existence, and struggling against life's natural expression. This is constant conflict.

It's important to note that none of this is a situation of anyone doing anything wrong. There is no one doing anything wrong, because there is no one doing anything. The natural flow of life gives everyone the fantasy of a self that is separate from existence, the fantasy of a self that is understanding and controlling existence.

We start out being the simple, warm, vibrant happening of this moment, and, soon after that, the focus goes on a deluded fantasy that contains confusion, frustration, and emotional turmoil. Life naturally gives everyone this fantasy, this confusion, conflict, and emotional distress.

The fantasy of "self" that is understanding and controlling life, and the emotional conflict that it brings with it, never disrupts the natural flow of existence; it is simply part of the natural flow.

The Way Out of Delusion

So, the question naturally arises, how can we get out of this fantasy of being someone who is understanding and directing existence?

How do we get out of it, so that we no longer suffer the conflict, frustration, struggle, and despair that it brings?

The answer is amazingly simple. If we are interested in getting out of it, we merely need to examine our experience of life and realise three simple facts:

1. There is only the happening of this moment.
2. There is no way of saying what this happening is.
3. There is no one making anything happen.

There is only the happening of this moment

Again, if I were to ask you why you feel that you are existing, you would say that it's because it feels like something is happening right now.

That's our only feeling of existing, the feeling that something is happening now.

Does this happening feel like the past or the future, or does it feel like the happening that we call now?

Of course, it feels like the happening we call now. We can ask this question a million times and the answer will always be the same. It always feels like the happening of now.

There is no experience of a past or a future, because the past and future don't really exist. They have never existed. They only exist in thinking, in imagination.

The only thing that is ever experienced is the feeling of the warm, vibrant happening of this moment.

Time does not exist. There is no past or future in our actual experience; there is only this immediate feeling of something happening, right now.

If you see this clearly, you'll realise why Stephen Hawking, and Albert Einstein would always say that time is an illusion.

If we want to explore life clearly, we cannot explore it through the past or the future, because those things don't exist. They are merely things that we imagine.

Exploring your past cannot give you an understanding of what you are, or what life is. The past is a fantasy that doesn't exist anywhere other than in imagination, in memory.

The only thing that we can explore is the actual happening of this moment. There is the feeling of the warm, vibrant happening of this moment. That's all that is ever existing.

There is no way of saying what this happening is

Again, if I were to ask you what this warm, vibrant happening is, you don't have any way of saying what it is. You have words that point to different portions of this happening, but those words don't tell you what this really is.

As a baby, you didn't know what the happening of this moment is, and you still don't know what this happening is.

More than that, this happening isn't even what it looks like.

It looks like it is static, unchanging, shapes, forms, and patterns, but our entire experience of these shapes, forms, and patterns is that they're changing.

This moment is like a cloud that is always moving and shifting in its appearance, a cloud of unknowing, because there is no way of saying what any of it actually is.

Every shape, form, and pattern, that we know of, has changed in our experience.

Our thoughts, moods, bodies, actions, relationships, and so on, have always been changing. The cities we live in are always changing; the movement of nature is always flowing; the climate is shifting; the surface of the planet moves, creating earthquakes; the weather shifts; the planet turns on its axis and orbits the sun. The Milky Way Galaxy spirals in space, and the universe, the one big turning, is constantly moving, shifting, and expanding.

If we sit quietly, doing nothing, the warm vibrant process that we are makes itself obvious. The breath comes and goes, the heart beats. There are pulsations, vibrations, little waves of energy, a little twinge here, a little shift there. Thoughts come and go, sounds come and go, moods come and go, urges come and go. Eventually an urge arises that compels us to stand up, to do something else, and we move to other activities.

This is life as we experience it, a changing, moving, shifting, flowing event, always moving on to some other appearance. This is the movement of creation, endlessly forming, never becoming anything in particular.

But it's not changing in any chaotic way; it has a natural way of becoming itself in each moment.

A rose becomes a rose, a squirrel becomes a squirrel. We can see the natural flow of existence forming itself in every moment. The flow of light and dark, hot and cold, the changing of the weather, the climate, the seasons, the evolution of animals and people, the constant appearance of shapes, forms and, patterns, endlessly becoming new shapes, forms, and patterns.

As Nietzsche pointed out, it is the dance of endless becoming.

The warm, vibrant, unexplainable, happening that you are, the vibrant happening that existence is, is happening right now.

It's the feeling of the warm, vibrant happening of this moment.

There is no way of saying what this happening is. It has no actual name and it has no actual form.

No one is making anything happen

Are you making yourself happen?

The process that you are is happening right now. You can feel the warm, vibrant, happening that you are. Just close your eyes and feel the happening.

Are you making yourself happen?

Make no effort at all, simply relax, and rest. Do you stop happening? Or do you go on happening, without any effort?

Sometimes it seems that we make things happen. We go get a pizza or plan a career. But, if we look at those activities closely, we can realise that we have an urge to do those things; we want to do those things, and many other things.

As Schopenhauer pointed out, we can do what we want to do, but we don't create our wants. We never create our wants. We never create the urge to do something.

Those urges simply arise as a movement of nature, the universe. So, all of our doing is not our doing: it's the doing of nature, the doing of the universe.

We don't create our wants, our urges, and we don't create our bodies and brains that are moved by those wants and urges.

There is no self that is making anything happen. There is simply the warm, vibrant happening of this moment, happening the way it happens. We are this unexplainable happening.

The most important aspect of this is that everything has a built-in, formative urge.

The universe, the one movement, has an automatic urge to form itself the way it does, in each moment.

We can see this everywhere. It's obvious. The clouds form and move the way they do. The weather forms and moves the way it does. The seasons form and shift the way they do.

Everything moves through its natural cycles, its

natural urges. Plants grow without deciding to grow. Animals reproduce without deciding to reproduce. Everything simply happens the way it happens.

We don't believe a squirrel is deciding to be a squirrel or deciding to do the things that it does. We feel that it is always being the only thing it can be in any moment.

We don't believe that a squirrel is making career choices to direct its career as a squirrel. Stars, and tomato plants, don't direct their lives. Neither does anything else in existence. But for some strange reason, we believe that we decide what we're going to be and what we're going to do.

Even though we know that we don't create our body and brain and we are not making them operate the way they operate.

We can do the things we want to do, but we don't create our wants and we don't create the body or brain that is moved by those wants. All of that is the movement of nature.

The truest sense of ourselves, and the truest sense of existence, comes when we simply feel the happening of this moment.

There isn't even a "feeler" feeling the happening. There's just the feeling of this immediate, warm, vibrant occurrence.

All of our descriptions of life are deluded interpretations. We have our clearest sense of life when we are not focused on thinking. An obsessive focus on thinking merely confuses everything. It brings fragmentation, conflict, and a deluded, useless struggle against the natural movement of existence, a struggle against its natural order.

The obsessive belief that descriptions of form are an accurate view of existence, brings an extreme mental conflict, and despair, that may not be necessary, if you realise that all the descriptions of life are deluded.

If we acknowledge a few obvious facts of life, very clearly, then all of our delusions will be realised to be delusions.

In our experience, all there is is the warm, vibrant happening of this moment, presenting itself, automatically. There is no self that is separate from this happening, no self making any of it happen, and there is no self that is directing it.

There is no way to say what this moment actually is. There's just what's happening and it has its own way of happening.

There is just the feeling of it happening and everything that you are, everything that you need to be and do, simply happens, automatically.

Do not observe the happening of this moment, because that's delusion.

The idea that there is a you observing this moment is a fantasy.

If you believe the false idea, that you are observing life, the focus is already lost in a fragmented, conflicted delusion.

Even the thought that there is a "feeler" feeling the happening is a delusion.

There is simply something happening, right now, so simply be this happening, and your life will unfold in its fullest way, without being lost in deluded stories.

Life is the unexplainable happening of this moment, endlessly becoming what it has to be in each moment.

This action, this movement, this spontaneous happening, is all that ever exists. It is the feeling of the warm, vibrant happening of this moment.

The false story that we are an observer observing life, separates us from what we really are.

The focus on a label, or a description, of any kind, puts the focus on cold, fragmented thoughts, and not on the full, warm, unexplainable happening that actually exists.

The false belief that thought can understand and

direct existence brings conflict, and the subsequent actions, based on those delusions, are aggressive and controlling.

We attempt to control our behaviour, wishing we were something different. We attempt to suppress our thoughts, moods, and actions, as well as the thoughts, moods, and actions of others. And when that fails, we make more violent attempts to suppress, and oppress, ourselves, and others.

The focus on deluded descriptions misses the miracle of life's event.

Everything is simply given in the happening of this moment. Everything is always the correct expression of nature, the universe.

Not all thinking is harmful. Some of it is useful, but all of it is in conflict with the life we actually experience.

How Can We Live Without Thinking?

We don't have to live without thinking. Thinking is a very natural portion of the movement of existence, and it is useful in certain situations.

But thinking is always in conflict with our experience of life; it is always a distorted interpretation of life, and if we realise that fact, very clearly, we don't have to cling to that deluded, conflicted interpretation.

We also don't have to live with the frustration, despair, and useless struggle that the delusion brings with it.

If we are interested, we can explore our experience of this moment in a very clear way, and realise some very simple facts. There is only the happening of this moment. There is no way to say what this happening is. There is no one making anything happen.

All of this is obvious, from our actual experience of life, the experience of this moment.

Whatever this happening is, it is always moving to its natural order, and it is always, automatically, expressing every apparent thing as fully as it can. This includes us.

Birds and flowers don't make themselves happen and they don't have to worry about directing their lives. All of that is taken care of, because they don't create themselves, or their actions.

A daisy doesn't have to worry about what to do in life. It doesn't have to understand itself or direct its behaviour. It's a movement of creation, always becoming what it has to be. Always fulfilling its formative urge.

Birds and flowers have a natural destiny. They are always unfolding in the only way they can, the only way that they're expressed by nature.

It's not really a situation of birds and flowers following their destiny, because it's always a completely unexplainable happening, simply happening the way it does. But this creative flow has the appearance of various forms, arising and passing, so we can say that those apparent forms have a destiny.

The movement of life has a directional formative urge, the urge to flow in a certain way, and that urge is always expressing every apparent thing in its fullest way, in every moment.

In the same way that the universe grows a flower, the universe automatically grows every apparent thing in existence, including us.

In the first recorded Zen teaching, the Buddha gathered a number of his followers together and, as they sat there, he simply held up a flower. That was all he did.

Only one of his monks, Mahakassapa, understood what he was pointing to, the mysterious happening of this moment, automatically growing everything, in the same way that it grows a flower.

Like the flower, we don't know what we are, or what life is, and, like the flower, we simply happen as a movement of nature.

Every apparent thing in existence has a built-in urge to become what it is and to do what it does, in any moment.

As Carl Rogers so beautifully pointed out, we have an actualising tendency, a formative urge. We are a process of creation endlessly becoming what it has to be in each moment, and then moving on to what it has to be in the next moment.

This is the movement of the universe, the one movement, the great spirit, the river of life, the unformed ocean of existence … always moving in its natural way.

It is the warm, vibrant, unexplainable happening of this moment.

If we realise this, in a clear way, then we drop the ridiculous notion that we are in charge of life, and stop telling everybody, including ourselves, what we should be.

Everything has to be exactly what it is in any moment, because nothing is making itself happen, including us.

Realising this, we can stop trying to understand and direct life, and start feeling how life is naturally expressing itself, feeling its natural happening, rather than trying to tell it to be something else.

This is what Rogers was ultimately pointing to. Instead of telling people what they should be, start listening to what they really are, to what they have to be.

Each one of us is a natural, and unique, expression of the universe.

Remember that no two apparent things in existence are identical. Each one of us has to be the uniquely different happening that we are; there is no option to that.

This is always a mysterious action of creation, moving to its natural formative urge, always fulfilling itself in every moment.

In realising this, we no longer see ourselves as someone separate from the happening. Instead, we simply feel the happening that we are, and find our wholeness, harmony, and rest in being that happening.

We find our real being, in the feeling of the happening of this moment, simply happening, with no way of saying what it is and no one making it happen.

We can throw away all the descriptions of life; every description that anyone has ever given is false. There is no way of saying what any of this is.

And we can throw away any idea of directing life.

Instead, there is the feeling of the warm, vibrant, creative happening that we are, happening automatically. We simply need to honour the happening that we are.

We can stop getting into ridiculous and useless arguments over whose explanation of existence is the correct one. They're all wrong.

We can stop objecting to all the other people in the world, stop telling them that they should be like us, because they can't be like us, and we can't be like them.

We can stop objecting to the way life is moving, because there isn't anyone making it move. That includes our own actions. There is no human being making anything happen.

We don't create ourselves, and therefore, we do not create anything else.

We may be able to drop the attachment to all of these absurd notions of understanding and personal doing, and stop placing ourselves in arrogant superiority, or inferiority, to anyone else.

We can stop parading ourselves as self-made beings. We have never done anything, to be the person that we are, or to act in the way that we act.

We can't take credit, or blame, for anything. All of that is deluded thinking.

In living our lives, we can realise that we have to be the expression that we are, in any moment, and that is the natural expression of the universe.

We are just as valid as any other expression of existence. We are just as valid, and natural, as the expression of any other so-called human being.

We can realise that we are a process of creative unfolding, always becoming what it has to be, always fulfilling its natural formative urge. We don't grow ourselves anymore than a tomato plant grows itself.

We are a process, a movement, unfolding in the only way it can, and we don't make that happen.

To find our true expression, and our natural direction, we simply have to be the warm, vibrant happening that we are, the warm vibrant happening of this moment, and in this happening, there will be urges to focus on certain things, urges to think certain things, urges to act in certain ways, and urges to engage with life in a certain way.

None of this is our doing; it simply happens. It's our unique and natural expression.

Everyone is different.

We have to be the unique expression that we are, in any moment, despite the fact that there will be many people telling us that we should be something else.

Those people are simply petty tyrants, telling us to behave a certain way, to believe certain things, always telling us that we should be like them.

To find our natural wholeness, harmony, and rest, we simply have to be this warm, vibrant, unexplainable happening that we are and feel what feels right to us, in any moment.

Feel what feels right, in a deep way. I'm not talking about superficial feelings, or emotions.

Each of us has a deep feeling of what feels right to us, what situations feel right, what situations feel wrong, what actions feel right, what actions feel wrong, what feels healthy, what does not feel healthy, what feels safe and what feels unsafe.

It doesn't matter what someone else is telling us we should be, each of us has a deep natural urge to live in a certain way, to focus on certain things, to approach life in a certain way.

We will unfold in the way that nature grows us and we will have to be whatever we are in any moment.

Maybe we can realise that everyone is different and we have to be the unique expression that we are.

The futile effort to get everyone to conform to one way of thinking, or one way of living, is an impossible task.

As the Taoists stated, a crane has long legs and a duck has short legs. To try to shorten the legs of a crane or lengthen the legs of a duck, will only cause them pain. Nothing more than pain can come from that type of useless struggle against the natural flow of existence.

Perhaps we can realise that what we need to offer others is validation for who they are, to honour and respect the natural expression that they have to be.

Instead of condemning others, perhaps we can start respecting the diverse expressions of nature.

Instead of telling everyone that they should be something different to what they are, perhaps we can finally take an interest in the unique, and different, expression that they are. The expression that they have to be.

And, instead of believing that our own expression is somehow wrong, perhaps we can realise that we are the warm, vibrant, unexplainable happening of this moment, always becoming what it has to be. Always being the correct expression of life.

We don't need to understand anything, or make

anything happen. It feels like you are the warm, vibrant happening of this moment. Just be this happening.

You will automatically be all that you can be, because there has never been a "self" that is making anything happen.

There is only the warm, vibrant happening of this moment, always moving to its formative urge, always becoming what it has to be.

Not thinking gives the truest sense of what we are.

Dropping the focus on thought is where we find our wholeness, harmony, and rest.

The obsessive belief that thinking is bringing understanding and harmony to life, is a massive delusion.

Thinking cannot understand the experience of life; it is always in direct conflict with that experience. It cannot bring harmony; it is always in conflict with our actual experience of life.

The simple feeling that something is happening in this moment is the clearest sense of existence that anyone can possibly have.

We have the clearest sense of ourself, and life, when not thinking.

In simply resting, we find the happening that we are, and we will be compelled to do whatever we do, as an expression of nature, the universe, the great spirit, the river of life, this unformed ocean of existence.

Everything that we are, and everything that we will do, is compelled to happen.

Thinking is useful in a small number of ways, but thinking is never understanding, or directing, the happening of life. There is only the warm, vibrant, unexplainable happening of this moment, happening the way it is happening. Nothing else exists.

It feels like something is happening, right now. Simply be this happening.

You can't know yourself as anything in particular; everything is changing.

You can't observe yourself; that's a delusion.

The fullest, truest sense of what you are, and what existence is, is the feeling of this immediate, warm, vibrant happening. The feeling of thoughts coming and going, moods coming and going, breath coming and going, pulsations, vibrations, waves of energy, and so on. And urges coming and going. Urges to move, urges to think, urges to act, in various ways.

Just be this happening, endlessly becoming what it has to be, in any moment.

Endnote

If you are having difficulty relating to the fact that everything is movement, there are two activities you might want to explore.

The first is to buy some incense and then sit in a way that you can watch the smoke rising up from the incense, after you light it.

Focus on the moving smoke. Then think of any "thing" that you can think of. It could be the weather, a cat, a house, an emotion, a body, and so on, any "thing" at all.

Ask yourself whether, in your experience, that thing changes. Watch the smoke as you consider whether every thing changes, or not, considering your experience of life. Consider as many "things" as you possibly can, one after the other.

The second activity you might want to explore is to get online, watching every time-lapse video that you can possibly watch, while considering what those videos are revealing.

Anyone interested in the similarities between the Buddha's description of conceptual viewpoints, and the descriptions that modern researchers offer, can refer to another of my books, titled *Buddhessence*.

Acknowledgments

An entire lifetime has gone into the expression of this one small book.

I want to thank my mother, Gwen, my father, Ed, and my brother, Brent, for their years of support. The most that anyone can offer to another person is the loving acceptance of who they are.

Even though this book is simply expressing my experience of life, there are many others that I want to acknowledge as, in some way, being part of this.

Jiddu Krishnamurti, Ruth Denison, Robert Adams, Ajahn Sumedho, Ramesh Balsekar, U.G. Krishnamurti, Philip Guston, Agnes Martin, Carl Rogers, George Washington Carver, Bob Dylan, and Muhammad Ali.

Sally Shea Murphy, Link Philips, Dale Purvis, Keith Millan, Dianne Wilt, Marcus Fellowes, Mary Wall, Ross Davies, Robert Dean Keddie, Richard Kellie, Sandra Stuart, Jill Osler, Sheilagh Konyk, Nick Herzmark, Sally Perchaluk, Juliette Sabot, Malamarie Sinha, Norma

Nickson, Margaret and Billie Webster, Sophie Rondeau, Joan Tollifson, Bob Rogers, Doug Phillips, Michelange Quay, Toan Tran, Valerie Metcalfe, Jon Mousely, Dale Ingram, Jack Deyermendjian, Joe Forsyth, Sakti Rose, Jennifer Steen, Trevor Long, Lynn-Marie Harper, Enid Stevens, Julian Noyce, and Catherine Noyce.

There are many more, but I will stop there. If I don't, it will be a list of every apparent person that I have ever encountered.

CONVERSATIONS ON AWAKENING

Interviews by Iain and Renate McNay

Conversations on Awakening features 24 unique accounts of Awakening all taken from transcripts of interviews made for conscious.tv.

Some of the interviewees are renowned spiritual teachers while others are completely unknown having never spoken in public or written a book.

These conversations will hopefully encourage you, inspire you, and maybe even guide you to find out who you really are.

Conversations on Awakening: Part One features interviews with A.H Almaas, Jessica Britt, Sheikh Burhanuddin, Linda Clair, John Butler, Billy Doyle, Georgi Y. Johnson, Cynthia Bourgeault, Gabor Harsanyi, Tess Hughes, Philip Jacobs and Igor Kufayev.

 ***Conversations on Awakening: Part Two*** features interviews with Susanne Marie, Debra Wilkinson, Richard Moss, Mukti, Miek Pot, Reggie Ray, Aloka (David Smith), Deborah Westmorland, Russel Williams, Jurgen Ziewe, Martyn Wilson and Jah Wobble.

Published by White Crow Books.
Available from Amazon in ebook and paperback format and to order from all good bookstores.

Part one: p.282, ISBN: 978-1786770936
Part two: p.286, ISBN: 978-1786770950

www.conscious.tv

Books in print from New Sarum Press

Real World Nonduality—Reports From The Field; Various authors

The Ten Thousand Things by Robert Saltzman

Depending on No-Thing by Robert Saltzman

The Joy of True Meditation by Jeff Foster

'What the...' A Conversation About Living by Darryl Bailey

The Freedom to Love—The Life and Vision of Catherine Harding by Karin Visser

Death: The End of Self-Improvement by Joan Tollifson

2020/21 Publications

Glorious Alchemy—Living the Lalita Sahasranama by Kavitha Chinnaiyan

Collision with the Infinite by Suzanne Segal

Transmission of the Flame by Jean Klein

The Ease of Being by Jean Klein

Open to the Unknown by Jean Klein

Yoga in The Kashmir Tradition (2nd Edition) by Billy Doyle

The Mirage of Separation by Billy Doyle

Looking Through God's Eyes by Han van den Boogaard

The Genesis of Now by Rich Doyle

Fly Free by Dami Roelse

Advaitaholics Anonymous by Shiv Sengupta

www.newsarumpress.com

Made in the USA
Las Vegas, NV
26 March 2021